ART DECO
Design & Ornament

Edited by Henri Rapin

Dover Publications, Inc.
Mineola, New York

Bibliographical Note

This Dover edition, first published in 2007, is a newly arranged compilation of all illustrations from the sixty-four plates included in the two volumes of *La sculpture décorative moderne,* published by Editions Charles Moreau, Paris. The first volume, subtitled *Première Série,* was published in 1925. The second edition, subtitled *Nouvelle Série* (but on its cover given a different title: *La sculpture décorative à l'exposition des arts décoratifs de 1925*), has no publication date.

DOVER *Pictorial Archive* SERIES

International Standard Book Number: 0-486-45431-2

Manufactured in the United States of America
Dover Publications, Inc., 31 East 2nd Street, Mineola, N.Y. 11501

Contents

Emile BERNAUX

Emile BERNAUX

Albert BINQUET

Albert BINQUET

Albert BINQUET

Albert BINQUET

Albert BINQUET

Henri BOUCHARD

Henri BOUCHARD

Henri BOUCHARD

10

Henri BOUCHARD

Marcel BOURAINE

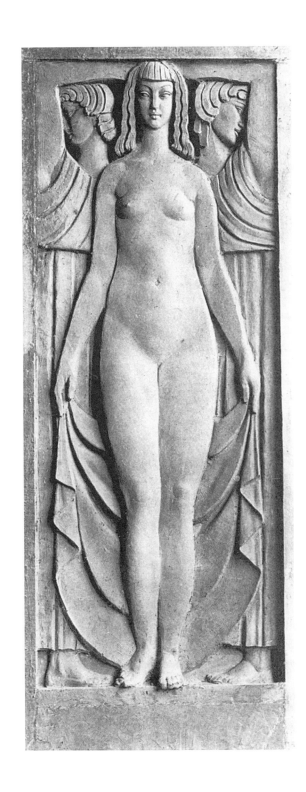 

Marcel BOURAINE and Pierre LE FAGUAYS   13

Emile-Antoine BOURDELLE

14

Emile-Antoine BOURDELLE

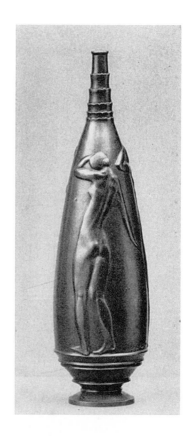

Edouard CHASSAING

Edouard CHASSAING

Georges de BARDYÈRE

18

Georges de BARDYÈRE

Matthieu GALLEREY

Jean-Baptiste GAUVENET

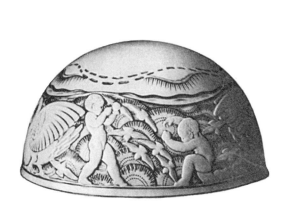

Albert GUÉNOT

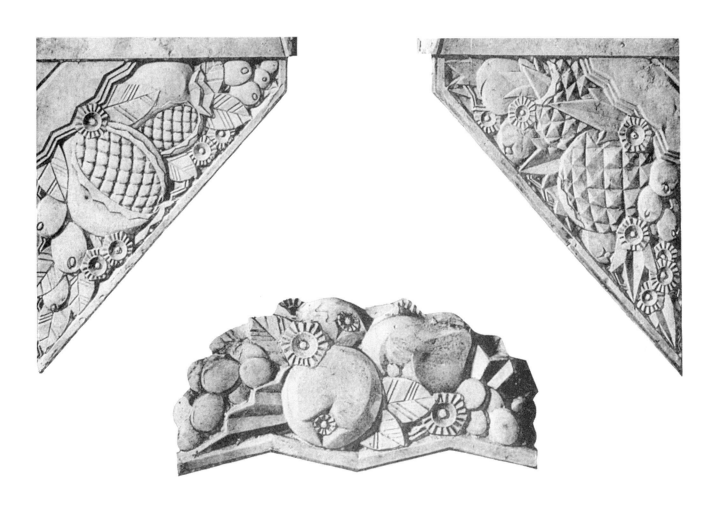

Albert GUÉNOT

Albert GUÉNOT

Charles HAIRON

27

Charles HAIRON

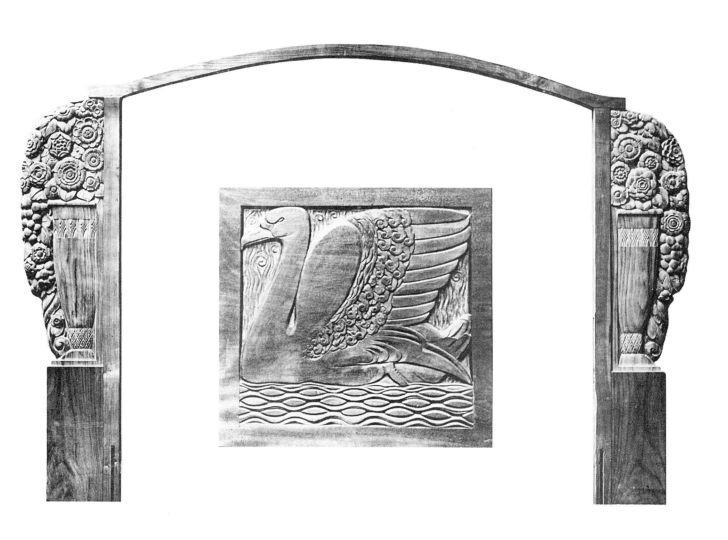

Charles HAIRON

Léon JALLOT

Léon JALLOT

Léon JALLOT

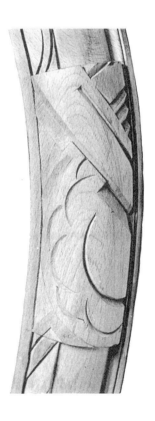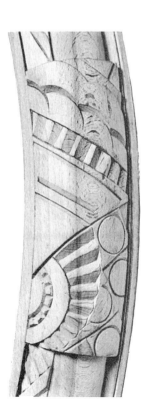

Léon JALLOT

34   Léon JALLOT

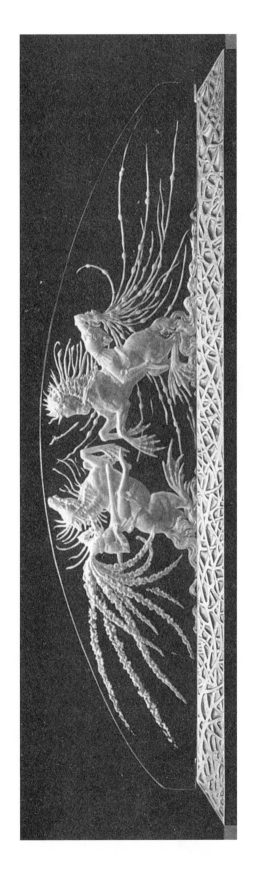

René-Jules LALIQUE

René-Jules LALIQUE

38   Gaston-Etienne LE BOURGEOIS

Gaston-Etienne LE BOURGEOIS

Gaston-Etienne LE BOURGEOIS

Gaston-Etienne LE BOURGEOIS

Gaston-Etienne LE BOURGEOIS

Laurent MALCLÈS

Laurent MALCLÈS

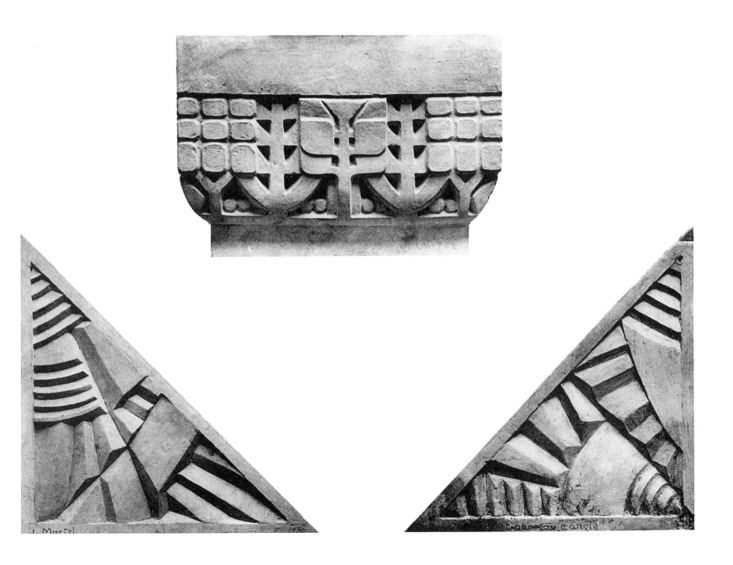

Joel and Jan MARTEL

48   Joel and Jan MARTEL

Max BLONDAT

Max BLONDAT

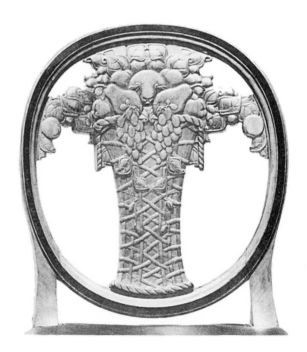

Paul FOLLOT

Louis SUE and André MARE   53

Louis SUE and André MARE

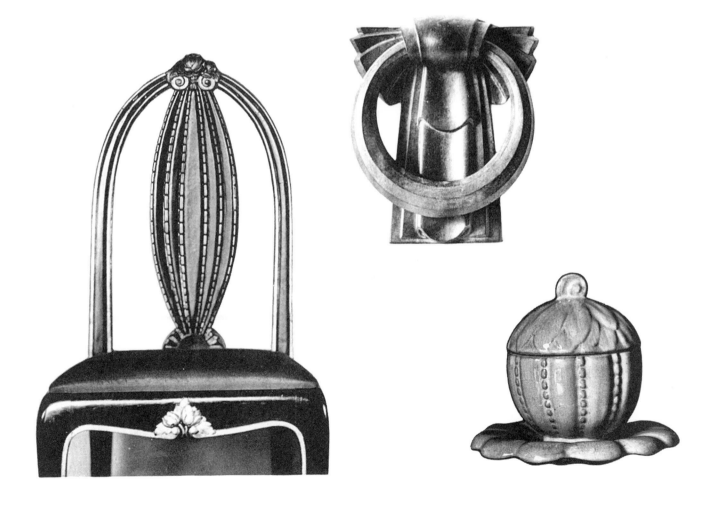

Louis SUE and André MARE

Louis SUE and André MARE   57

Top and bottom: Paul Bernard VÉRA and Jacques-Marie MARTIN
Center: Paul Bernard VÉRA and Pierre-Marie POISSON

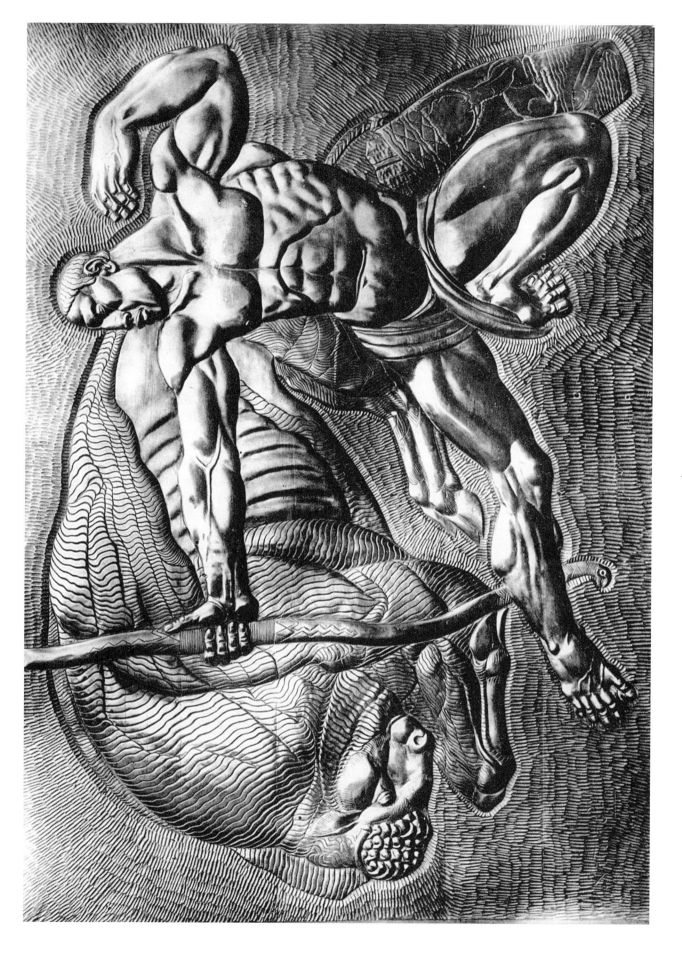

Georges ARTÉMOFF

Georges ARTÉMOFF

Alfred BOTTIAU

D. GÉLIN and Alfred BOTTIAU

D. GÉLIN and Alfred BOTTIAU

Henri BOUCHARD

Henri BOUCHARD

Henri BOUCHARD

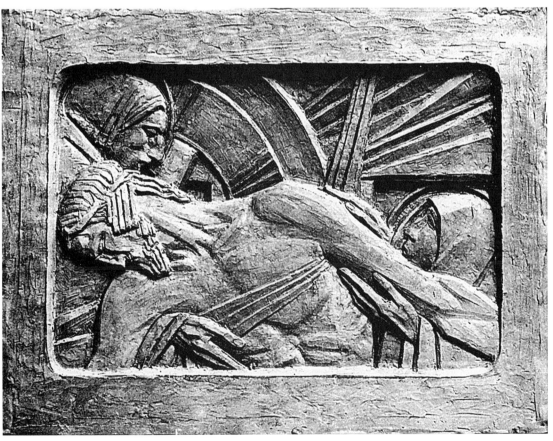

Henri BOUCHARD

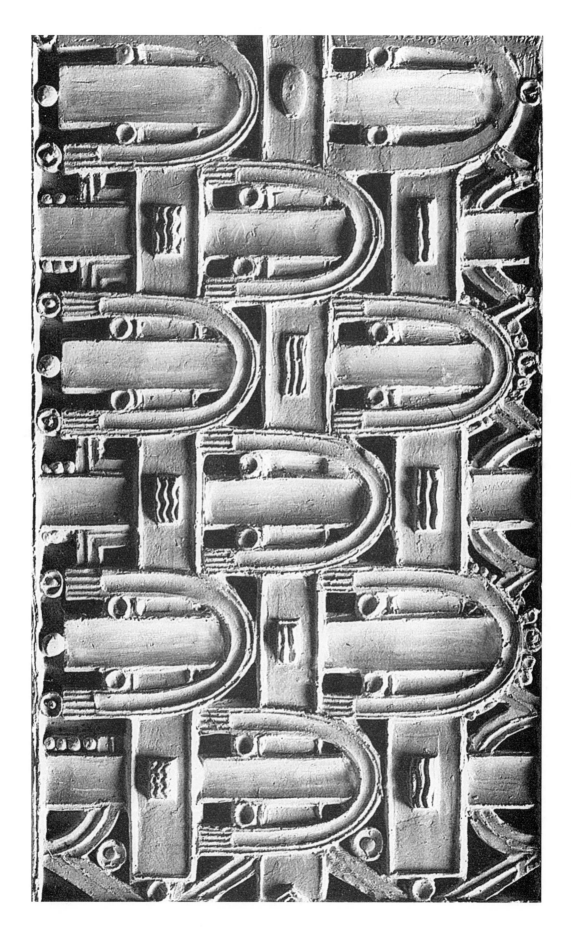

Jean DEBARRE

68

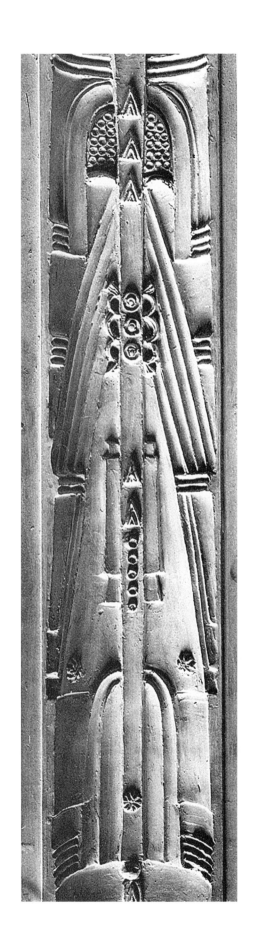

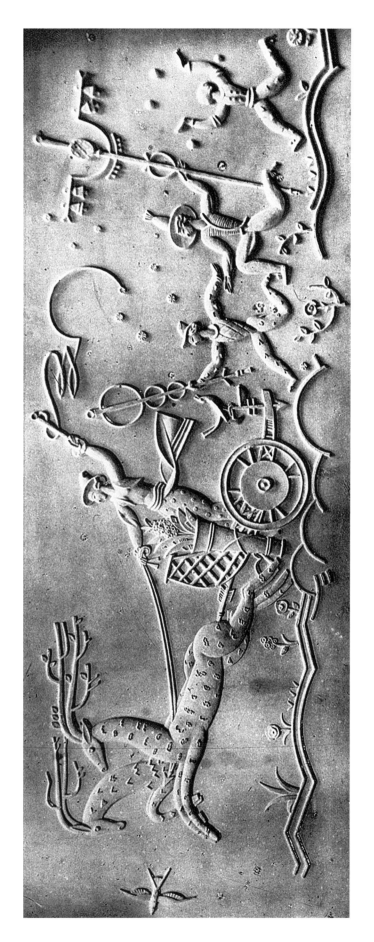

Jean DEBARRE

69

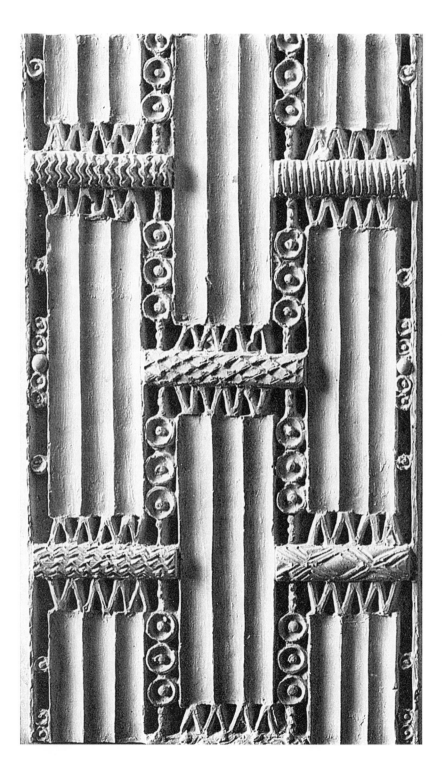

Jean DEBARRE

Jean DEBARRE

Jean DEBARRE

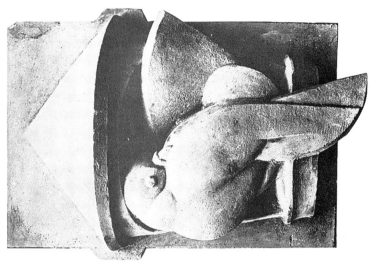

Jean DEBARRE

Jean DEBARRE

Jean DEBARRE

76   École Boulle

  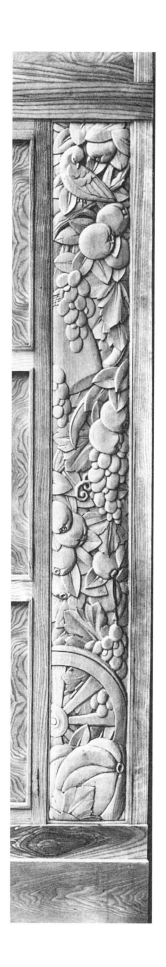

École Boulle

École Boulle

École Boulle

École Boulle

École Boulle

Albert GUÉNOT

82

Top: École Boulle

Bottom: École Nationale Supérieure des Arts Décoratifs

83

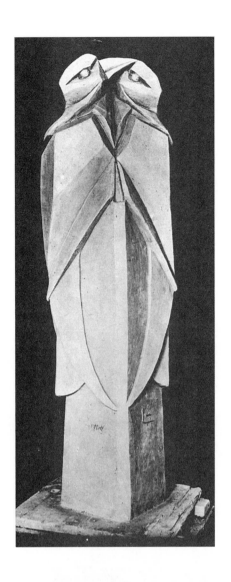

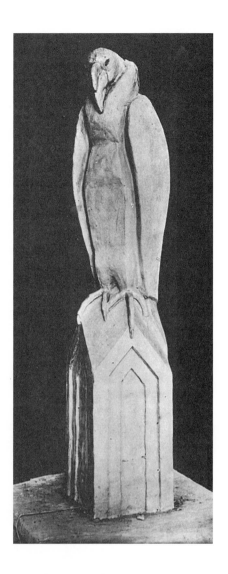

École Nationale Supérieure des Arts Décoratifs

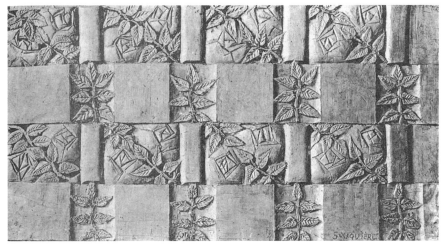

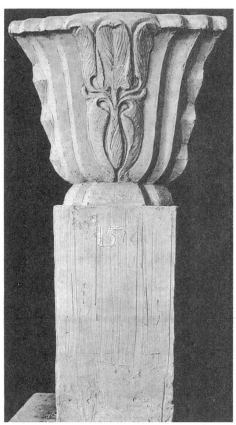

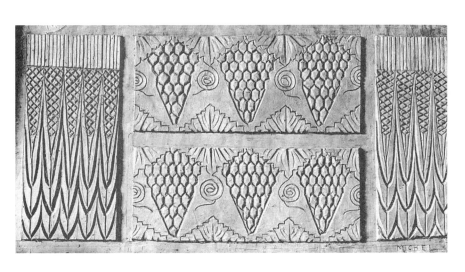

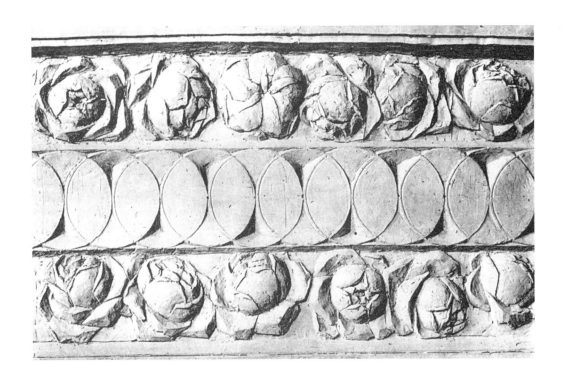

École Nationale Supérieure des Arts Décoratifs

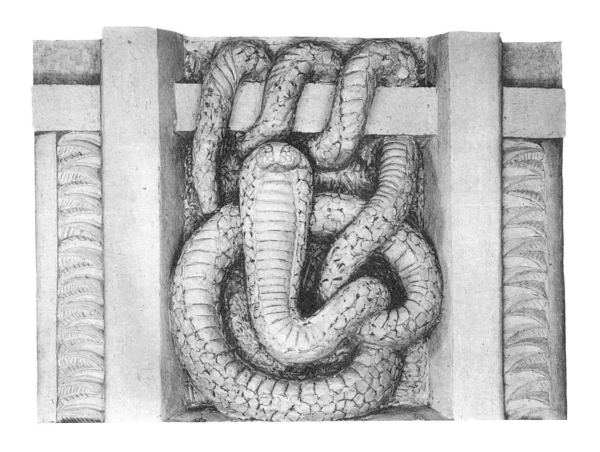

École Nationale Supérieure des Arts Décoratifs

École Nationale Supérieure des Arts Décoratifs

Camille GARNIER

Camille GARNIER

Camille GARNIER

Léon JALLOT

Léon JALLOT

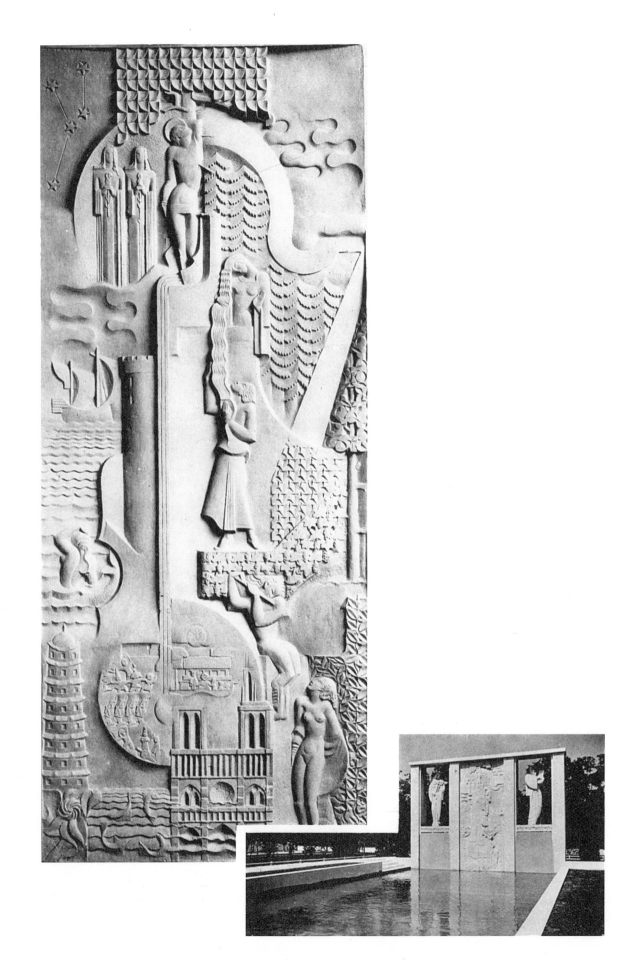

98   Joel and Jan MARTEL (Monument to Claude Debussy)

Joel and Jan MARTEL (Monument to Claude Debussy)   99

LE PREMIER SERVICE AERIEN
PARIS BUENOS-AIRES PARIS A ETE
REALISE EN MIL NEUF CENT TRENTE TROIS PAR
"L'ARC-EN-CIEL" AVEC L'EQUIPAGE
MERMOZ-CARRETIER-MAILLOUX-MANUEL JOUSSE
ET LE CONSTRUCTEUR RENE COUZINET

LES LAUREATES DU CONCOURS "POURQUOI J'AIME PARIS"
EN RECONNAISSANCE DE LA GENEREUSE INITIATIVE
DE MESSIEURS BADER, HEILBRONN ET MEYER

Docteur GEORGES DEQUIDT

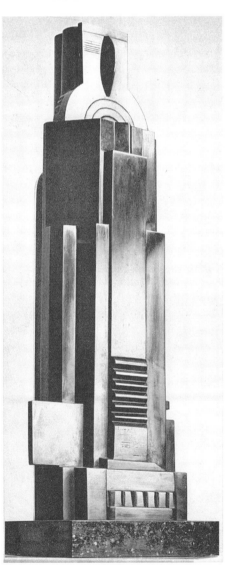

Gustave MIKLOS

Pierre-Marie POISSON (after compositions by Paul Bernard VÉRA)

Pierre-Marie POISSON (after compositions by Paul Bernard VÉRA)

103